895

LALIQUE

ALL COLOUR PAPERBACKS
Other titles include:

Erté
Mucha
Alma Tadema
Burne-Jones
Kate Greenaway
The Orientalists
The Liberty Style
Fashion Illustration
Poiret
Tiffany
Decorative Stained Glass

THE GLASS OF RENE LALIQUE
LALIQUE

A RIZZOLI PAPERBACK

Introduction by
VICTOR ARWAS

RIZZOLI
NEW YORK

Frontispiece
Douze figurines avec bouchon – bottle moulded in relief with six pairs of nude dancing figures, the stopper moulded as a kneeling nude, 29 cms.

I should like to thank Cobra, London for providing the illustrations for Plates 1–6 and 8–12, and Gallery 1925, London for allowing us to photograph items for Plates 17–24, 27, 31, 33 and 35. Plates 25, 29 and 30 are from private collections and all other items are from Editions Graphiques Gallery, London.

First published in the United States of America in 1980 by
RIZZOLI INTERNATIONAL PUBLICATIONS, INC.
712 Fifth Avenue/New York 10019

Library of Congress Catalog Card Number 79-92368
ISBN 0-8478-0282-5

Printed and bound in Hong Kong

INTRODUCTION

Though best known for his innovative glass ware in the Art Deco style, René Lalique first made his name as a jeweller in the 1890s. He constantly experimented, using a wide variety of materials and techniques to produce his fantastic designs in the form of naiads, mermaids, chimeras and dragonflies – and he was soon the darling of the smart, wealthy avant-garde set in Paris. Even then he was interested in glass and began to incorporate it in some of his jewellery, using glass studs as jewels or engraving a coloured glass or clear crystal section with landscapes, plants or a woman's face. He also used glass in some of his multi-media sculptures.

The 1900 Paris Universal Exhibition was a great triumph for Lalique and his jewellery – but already he was looking for new fields to conquer. In 1902 he rented a small workshop at Clairefontaine, near Rambouillet, equipped it and hired four glass workers. His interest in glass was, from the first, in its sculptural aspect. Using the *cire-perdue*, or lost wax process, he would model individual figures, or vase shapes decorated in high relief with figures, plants, etc. in wax. A mould was then cast around the wax model and molten glass poured into the mould. The wax model melted away, the moulded glass model replaced it and, once annealed, was a unique cast. Lalique's *cire-perdue* glass was, however, glass and should not be confused with *pâte-de-verre*. His early *cire-perdue* glass is rarely signed, although some were occasionally marked with the imprint of his thumb in the soft wax, which was reproduced in the glass mould.

In 1907 François Coty commissioned Lalique to design some labels for his perfume bottles. He designed not only the labels but the bottles. These first perfume bottles were executed in the glassworks of Legras & Cie. The following year Lalique rented the Verrerie de Combs-la-Ville, a glassworks at Combs (Seine-et-Marne) and purchased it a year later. More perfume bottles were commissioned from him over the years, from Coty as well as many other perfume manufacturers such as Worth, Orsay and Roger & Gallet. They were all produced in his own glass works.

His first all-glass exhibition was held in Paris in 1912 and the following year he ceased producing precious jewellery. After the First World War, in 1918, Lalique purchased his second glass works, a large factory at Wingen-sur-Moder (Bas-Rhin), close to the German border. Lalique was then fifty-eight years old and about to embark on a new career. He was determined to produce fine quality glass using modern industrial techniques capable of a degree of mass-production without the loss of quality. Some of his glass was blown into moulds. This traditional technique involved considerable experimentation in creating the right type of mould, for Lalique designed vessels decorated at times in very high relief. Some of his glass was produced in the stamping press, a technique he pioneered.

Unique vessels, plaques and panels were still occasionally produced by the *cire-perdue* method of casting, and this technique was also used to produce more permanent moulds which were reusable and could thus be used to produce several examples of the moulded glass. Its major advantage over other mould-making processes was that it produced moulds of exceptional quality, capable of reproducing the subtlest detail, however fine or shallow, in the wax model.

Lalique produced an enormous range of articles in glass. These included vases, bowls, trays, ashtrays, saucers, clock cases, decanters, jugs, glasses and tumblers. Table glass included lemonade and wine sets of decanters or jugs with glasses. Chunky models were moulded with modernistic designs, while wine glasses were frequently blown into moulds in very thin-walled glass which was then often engraved with a decorative pattern. Lamps came in a variety of designs, some table lamps with glass bases and shades or metal (frequently chromed) bases. Many different ceiling fittings were also produced, moulded bowls strung on thick cords or chains, often with matching wall fittings. He also designed elaborate electroliers with shaped glass panels moulded with designs strung together to form circular patterns, sometimes at several levels, rather like geometric birds' nests.

Glass jewellery was produced in a number of shapes. Moulded pendants of coloured or colourless glass in the form of buttons, crosses, T-shapes, O-shapes and shield shapes were strung on knotted neck cords with tassels. Other moulded glass pebbles were mounted in gilt metal to form brooches. Glass beads were strung as long necklaces, while oblong ones were strung as bracelets on elastic cord.

Wall-cladding, illuminated decorative panels, tables and doors were all made in massive pressed glass. Statuettes were designed either to stand decoratively or in conjunction with a base containing a concealed light which illuminated the figure. These bases were sometimes made of marble, but more usually of bronze, either in a plain geometric shape or decorated with an appropriate design, cast in Lalique's own foundry. Nude nymphs with long hair, a graceful figure of *Suzanne au Bain* inspired by the Biblical story of Susannah and the elders, St. Geneviève the Patron Saint of Paris, as well as a host of other saintly figures, large fan shaped panels decorated with nude women or mermaids, knights on horseback jousting in a tournament or a startling chimera, were all made to fit illuminated plinths, as were some spectacular moulded vases.

The metal of Lalique's glass has frequently been criticised, particularly by English writers, as being rough and undistinguished. E. M. Elville, writing in his *English Table Glass* (1951) declares: 'Lalique's fame ... depended more on his ability as a mould maker than that of glass-maker, for his metal left much to be desired.' An opposite opinion is expressed by Guillaume Janneau who wrote: 'Lalique's glass has the ethereal brilliance of Arctic ice. Its texture is hardly visible and one can scarcely believe that it was once a thick, opaque substance, shaped by running into a mould; it would seem rather to consist of immaterial ether, the frozen breath of the Polar night.'

What may well have disturbed certain critics was the fact that Lalique deliberately chose not to use lead crystal, despite its purity, but to use a more malleable and responsive demi-cristal. Most of his creations are made from clear, uncoloured glass, the shape and design alone creating the impact. He occasionally used coloured glass: brown, red, green, blue, grey, yellow or black. Whenever a particular model was produced in coloured glass it was invariably also produced in a colourless version. Coloured Lalique glass is, however, both rare and very attractive and thus eagerly sought after by collectors. Lalique also created a different type of surface colouring by dipping a completed moulded vessel (in colourless or palely coloured glass) into a specially mixed paint. The vessel was then wiped clean on its protruding sections, the dipped colour being allowed to remain in the interstices, darkening and colouring highlights of the design. He even occasionally used more than one colour in this way on a single vessel. Lalique also used a subtle opalescent glass for some models, varying from pale blue to rich brown, depending on the direction and intensity of the light reaching it.

Some Lalique models have strong Art Nouveau designs, particularly in the characteristic use of nymphs with long hair, or mermaids with expressive tails. Others are more characteristically Art Deco, with geometric friezes of birds, figures or plants and rigorously zig-zag patterns in both shape and decoration.

The 1925 Paris International Exhibition of Decorative and Industrial Arts was, like the 1900 Exhibition, a great triumph for Lalique. His works were displayed in both his own pavilion and that of the Manufacture de Sèvres. For both pavilions Lalique designed a dining room which displayed a full range of his table-ware and lighting. The most stunning feature of the Sèvres pavilion was the illuminated ceiling which was divided into small opal glass panels by moulded glass divisions. Lalique also designed a monumental fountain which was placed in front of the Cour des Métiers pavilion. Set on a star-shaped base, a slender, phallic glass column rose skyward and when turned on the water jets shot out from nozzles placed all around the column up its entire height.

A whole new range of designs were introduced by Lalique at this exhibition, including an opalescent vase moulded with budgerigars, a chunky vase very deeply moulded with arabesques whose outside surface was enamelled black to contrast with the transparent body of the vase, and vases and boxes moulded with fish, mermaids and dragonflies. He had created a completely new style of glassware which soon became very fashionable and it was inevitable that cheaper versions would appear from other glassmakers. Some were abject copyists, producing marginal variations of Lalique models. Others were to create their own designs, frequently original and attractive.

During the 1930s a new type of glass ornament was manufactured by Lalique: the car mascot. Cars were becoming sleeker, faster, ever more elegant and an appropriate mascot forming a mast-head on the bonnet was essential. Lalique produced a series of mascots moulded to various designs, and set into a brass cap which both connected the mascot to the radiator cap and served to conceal a shaped two-coloured transparent filter, a light bulb, and wiring which was connected to the dynamo. Thus, when the car was in motion the mascot was illuminated through the colour filter, which provided a changeable light which was especially effective at night. His two most spectacular mascots were the figure of *Victoire*, now commonly known as the *Spirit of the Wind*, a woman's head straining forward, open mouthed, her geometrically aligned hair streaming back; and the *Libellule*, a large, aerodynamic dragonfly, poised hovering over the bonnet, its wings pointing firmly skyward. Other attractive mascots included a couple of finely modelled horses' heads, a ram's head, a peacock's head and a fine figure of a nude nymph straining backwards called *Vitesse*. Rather less attractive were the flat figures, circular medallions moulded in intaglio with a kneeling figure of a male archer or a St. Christopher, an amusing tailed comet, a greyhound or a group of five leaping horses. Modelled in the round were a falcon, a swooping swallow, a cockerel, a fish, etc. There was also a somewhat sinister eagle's head, reputedly fitted by Hitler's officers to their cars. The mascots are normally found in clear glass, sometimes highlighted by black staining in the interstices. They are occasionally found in smoky, opalescent or lightly tinted glass. They are fairly rare and much sought after. All are signed 'R. Lalique', either moulded on the side or engraved or acid-etched on the base.

With the exception of tiles, beads, certain panels and parts of lamps, all Lalique glass is signed. The earliest vases and models were signed 'R. Lalique France' in a fine copperplate script with a model number, the whole engraved on the rim of the base. Popular models were produced over a number of years, the moulds remaining in storage until required again. Later pressings of early models abandoned the earlier script signature with model number in favour of whatever signature was currently in use. Numbering was abandoned after about the middle 1920s, and signatures changed. The 'R. Lalique' in capital letters was either moulded in shallow relief on the base or acid-etched using a template. In the latter case it is sometimes barely visible to the naked eye.

In 1937 Lalique closed down his small Combs-la-Ville glass works and in 1940 when the German forces again occupied Paris and a large part of France, his factory at Wingen-sur-Moder was taken over by them. Lalique was then eighty years old. He died five years later on May 5th, 1945, shortly after the Liberation. His son, Marc Lalique, who had been in charge of production and the business side from the 1920s, took over the firm in 1945. While earlier models have continued to be produced (and, indeed, some early models are revived every year) many new designs are also launched. Tinted, coloured and opalescent glass were abandoned, as was surface colouring, in favour of a clearer and purer metal than in the past. All post 1945 glass is clearly marked 'Lalique France' without the use of the initial 'R' (it is, however, worth noting that some bowls produced in the 1930s were also signed just 'Lalique' in an incised script). In the 1970s Marc Lalique reintroduced the use of coloured glass, but this time in conjunction with colourless glass, and used sparingly and effectively for contrast.

From *Glass, Art Nouveau to Art Deco* by Victor Arwas, Academy Editions 1977.

1

Canarina – scent bottle moulded with a continuous pattern of eyes, the stopper fitted with a dropper, 5 cms.

2

Flacon cigales – glass scent bottle moulded with four crickets, 13 cms.

3

Poésie d'Orsay – bullet-shaped scent bottle moulded with a frieze of dancers, 14.5 cms. Made for d'Orsay.

4

Ambre – black glass scent bottle moulded with four caryatids, one on each corner, 13 cms. Produced with different moulded patterns on the stopper, this model was designed for the firm of d'Orsay.

5

Flacon quatre soleils – moulded glass scent bottle, 7 cms. This type of bottle was designed about 1912 and made over a period of several years. Not designed for any particular scent or scent manufacturer, they were intended for the dressing table. Perfume, purchased in plain bottles with elaborate labels, was then decanted into little bottles such as this one and the one in the following illustration.

6

Flacon serpent – glass scent bottle moulded with the inter-twined body of a snake, 9 cms. The stopper is in the shape of the snake's head.

7

Dans la nuit – large perfume bottle moulded all over with stars in relief, the background stained midnight blue, the stopper moulded with a crescent and stars.

8

Scent bottle with the stopper moulded as a standing female figure, 9.5 cms. This model was designed for the firm of Arys.

9

Flacon panier de roses – glass scent bottle moulded as a flower basket with roses, 10 cms. The stopper is also in the form of a rose.

10

Scent bottle, the crescent-shaped stopper moulded in intaglio with wild roses. Other scent bottle stoppers were moulded with a variety of flowers and fruit.

11

Scent bottle with the sides angled inwards to frame a central panel shallow-moulded with a girl in profile. This model dates from about 1912 and was made for a perfume called La Belle Saison by Houbigant.

12

Le Jade – moulded green glass scent bottle made for Roger & Gallet, 8 cms.

13

Myosotis, no. 613 — flat vanity table bottle with stopper moulded as a kneeling nude, 23 cms. A full set consisted of three bottles in different sizes and a box. The three stoppers and lid finial were moulded with kneeling nudes in different positions.

14

Carafe plate deux danseuses – flat bottle, the central panel moulded with two nude Bacchanalian dancers, 36.5 cms. This particular example belonged to the Duchess of Marlborough, the former Gladys Deacon, who was painted by Boldini and Sargent and sculpted by Epstein.

15

Brule parfums sirènes – perfume burner moulded in relief with mermaids, the snuffer/cover moulded with flowers, 18 cms.

16

Assiette figurine et fleurs – amber coloured glass plate
moulded with a nude and flowers in relief, 17 cms. diameter.

17

Bouchon de radiateur comète – moulded glass car mascot. Car mascots were first introduced by Lalique in 1929 and about thirty different designs were produced. All the models could also be used as paperweights.

18

Faucon – car mascot moulded as a falcon.

19

Vitesse – moulded glass car mascot symbolising speed, 18.5 cms.

20

Perche – car mascot moulded as a perch, 18 cms.

21

Coq houdan – one of two cockerel models for car mascots, this one treated in a geometrical stylisation more suitable to lead crystal than the more usual demi-cristal used by René Lalique, 20 cms.

22

Tête d'aigle – car mascot moulded as an eagle's head, 11 cms. The legend goes that Hitler's officers used this mascot on their cars.

23

Cinq chevaux – car mascot moulded with a stylised group of five horses.

24

Presse-papier tête de paon – moulded glass peacock's head, here used as a paperweight but also used as a car mascot, 18 cms.

25

Group of glass pendants. These were moulded in glass of various colours with different motifs in relief or intaglio. The central pendant is a miniature scent bottle.

26

Oiseau de feu – fan-shaped glass plaque, the firebird intaglio-moulded, the details finished on the wheel, set into a bronze base chased with stylised butterflies, 43 cms. The electrified base is set with a red glass plaque which gives a reddish glow to the highlights in the firebird. Similar illuminated plaques were made with motifs of peacocks, fish, birds, knights in armour, flowers and sailing ships.

27

Naiade – moulded glass statuette, 13 cms.

28

Suzanne – moulded glass statuette set into an illuminated bronze base, 23 cms. The pair to this figure, a dancer going in the opposite direction, was called *Thaïs*.

29

Statuette grande nue longs cheveux, socle lierre sur socle bois – the tall figure in moulded smoky glass, set on a wooden base with Chinese patterns, was originally designed in about 1912, 41 cms.

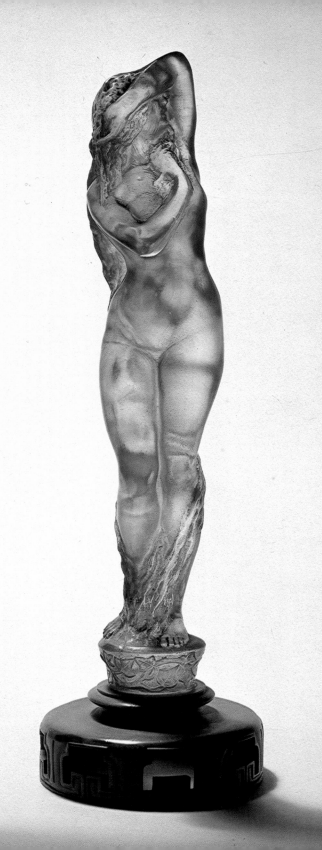

30

Salmonides – vase moulded with intertwined fish in relief, 29 cms.

31

Perruches – glass vase moulded with budgerigars, the outer surfaces polished, the inner ones not, 24 cms.

32

Camargue – massive vase with relief panels of wild horses in different attitudes, the glass partly polished and partly frosted, the panels stained, 29 cms.

33

Poissons — vase moulded with an overall pattern of fish, 24.5 cms.

34

Vase moulded with stylised acanthus leaves, the outer surfaces polished, the inner surfaces frosted, 23 cms.

35

Grenade – glass vase moulded with a scaly pattern inspired by the pomegranate.

36

Le Mans – brown glass vase moulded with a frieze of stylised cockerels, part of the design giving an opaque, mat finish, 10 cms.

37

Vase moulded with thistles in relief.

38

Sauterelles – vase deeply moulded with grasshoppers and leaves, the background stained blue, 27 cms

39

Avallon – vase moulded with birds in branches, 14.5 cms.

40

Archers – amber glass vase moulded in relief with a frieze of eagles and hunters, 26 cms.